low cost
cooking

Published by:
TYPHOON MEDIA CORPORATION

low cost
cooking

Low Cost Cooking
© TYPHOON MEDIA CORPORATION

Publisher
Simon St. John Bailey

Editor-in-chief
Susan Knightley

Prepress
Precision Prep & Press

Includes Index
ISBN 9781582796840
UPC 615269796849

2010

Printed in The United States

introduction

Most home cooks have to live within a budget. Whatever your household income, there are bills to be paid, treats to be planned and, of course, the weekly shopping to be done.

That's why we have created this exciting new cookbook. We firmly believe that low cost cooking should be enjoyable and successful. Cheap and cheerful really is possible.

low cost cooking
introduction

A few things to remember

• Fruit, vegetables and fish are much cheaper when they are in season and can be abundantly found. If they are out of season, it is more convenient to use canned food instead of paying for the fresh at the price of gold.

• Look for cheaper cuts of meat whenever possible. By using the right cooking method (usually slower cooking such as stewing) a cheap cut can provide great results.

• When shopping, follow these hints: try to leave the children at home so you're not "pressured" into unnecessary purchases; make a list and stick to it; never shop on an empty stomach.

- Use up leftovers rather than throwing them out. To avoid boring your family's palate, freeze the leftovers and serve them a couple of weeks later, or transform them into a different dish with a quick sauce or another smart touch.

- Do not dismiss the most expensive ingredients completely from your kitchen. The perfect solution for enjoying them without overspending is to incorporate them into your recipes in small amounts.

- Compare prices between different brands of the same product and choose the sales and special offers, particularly when you need to restock the fridge and the pantry.

- Never give up on a good presentation. Some herb sprigs or green leaves help you give a tempting look, even to the most humble of dishes.

Difficulty scale

■☐☐I Easy to do

■■☐I Requires attention

■■■I Requires experience

beetroot
timbales

■■□ | Cooking time: 50 minutes - Preparation time: 20 minutes

method

1. Purée the beetroot in a blender or food processor until smooth, measure 1 cup of purée, reserve remainder for another purpose.
2. Stir cream into the purée, pour mixture into a medium saucepan and stir over high heat until it boils. Reduce heat and simmer for 5 minutes; cool for 15 minutes.
3. Whisk eggs into beetroot mixture and pour into 4 greased, 1/2-cup capacity timbale tins. Cover with foil and stand in a baking tray filled with 2 cm/3/4 in of water. Bake timbales in a moderate oven for 45 minutes.
4. Heat extra cream and sour cream in a medium saucepan, over moderate heat, until sauce boils and reduces by a third. Stir in mustard and dill and serve with the timbales.

ingredients

> **480 g/15 1/2 oz canned baby beetroots, drained**
> **1/2 cup thickened cream**
> **4 eggs, lightly beaten**
> **3/4 cup thickened cream, extra**
> **1/4 cup sour cream**
> **1 teaspoon German mustard**
> **2 teaspoons chopped dill**

....
Serves 4

tip from the chef

Garnish with thin lemon slices and green sprigs, or with chopped hard-boiled egg and parsley leaves.

mustard
brussels sprouts

■□□ | Cooking time: 10 minutes - Preparation time: 5 minutes

ingredients
> **500 g/1 lb Brussels sprouts**
> **1 tablespoon butter**
> **1 tablespoon plain flour**
> **$1/2$ cup hot milk**
> **1 cup chicken stock**
> **2 teaspoons whole grain mustard**
> **1 tablespoon mayonnaise**

method
1. Bring a large saucepan of water to the boil, add Brussels sprouts and cook until just tender, about 10 minutes, drain.
2. Melt butter in a medium saucepan over moderate heat, add flour and mix well. Remove from heat, stir in milk and stock, return to heat and stir until sauce thickens. Stir in mustard and mayonnaise.
3. Pour sauce over Brussels sprouts, serve hot.

....

Serves 4

tip from the chef

This recipe results exquisite as a side dish for oven cooked meat.

onions
with dill butter

■□□ | Cooking time: 50 minutes - Preparation time: 5 minutes

method

1. Melt butter in a medium saucepan over moderate heat. Add garlic, cook for 1 minute.
2. Place onions in a baking dish and pour over 3/4 of the garlic butter. Bake in a moderate oven for 45 minutes or until cooked through.
3. Heat the remaining garlic butter again just before serving, stir in dill and brush over onions.

Serves 4

ingredients

> **100 g/3 1/2 oz butter**
> **3 cloves garlic, crushed**
> **8 small onions, halved**
> **1 tablespoon chopped fresh dill**

tip from the chef

To taste a delicious snack, shred the onions, mix them with sun-dried tomatoes and serve over toasts.

fennel
with tomato sauce

■□□ | Cooking time: 45 minutes - Preparation time: 15 minutes

ingredients

- > **2 medium fennel bulbs**
- > **2 tablespoons oil**
- > **2 tablespoons butter**
- > **2 cloves garlic, crushed**
- > **1 onion, chopped**
- > **1/2 cup chopped bacon, rind removed**
- > **2 tablespoons tomato paste**
- > **1 cup canned tomatoes**
- > **1/4 cup dry white wine**
- > **1 tablespoon dried basil**

method

1. Cut stalks from fennel and discard. Slice bulbs into wedges, about 2 cm/3/4 in thick; place in a lightly greased baking dish, brush with oil and bake in a moderate oven for 25 minutes.

2. Meanwhile, melt butter in a medium frying pan over moderate heat. Add garlic, onion and bacon, cook for 2 minutes. Add tomato paste, tomatoes, wine and basil and bring to the boil. Reduce heat and simmer for 15 minutes, stirring occasionally and breaking up the tomatoes with a wooden spoon.

3. Arrange a few wedges of fennel on each serving plate and spoon over the sauce.

....

Serves 4

tip from the chef
Serve as an starter, with poached eggs, or as an accompaniment for meat dishes.

cheddar
soufflé with vegetables

■ ■ □ | Cooking time: 25 minutes - Preparation time: 15 minutes

method

1. Melt butter in a medium saucepan over a moderately low heat. Add flour and cook for 1 minute, stirring constantly. Stir in hot milk and whisk over low heat until thick and smooth.
2. Remove from heat and cool for 10 minutes. Stir in cheese, nutmeg, egg yolks and chives, mix well.
3. Beat egg whites with an electric mixer until soft peaks form. Fold into cheese mixture, half a cup at a time.
4. Divide mixture between six ³/₄-cup capacity greased and collared soufflé dishes. Bake in a moderate oven for 15-20 minutes.
5. Boil vegetables until just tender. Serve with soufflé.

ingredients

- > 60 g/2 oz butter
- > ¹/₂ cup plain flour
- > 1¹/₄ cup hot milk
- > 1 cup grated mature Cheddar cheese
- > 1 teaspoon ground nutmeg
- > 3 eggs, separated
- > 2 tablespoons chopped chives
- > 1 red pepper, seeded, cut into strips
- > 2 medium carrots, cut into strips
- > 2 zucchini, cut into strips
- > 1 cup broccoli flowerets
- > chives for garnish

....
Serves 6

tip from the chef
Serve the soufflé immediately, as it flattens quickly once it has left the oven.

fettuccine
with pumpkin sauce

■□□ I Cooking time: 15 minutes - Preparation time: 10 minutes

ingredients
> **500 g/1lb fettuccine**
> **2 cups thickened cream**
> **$3/4$ cup cooked mashed pumpkin**
> **$1/4$ teaspoon ground black pepper**
> **$1/2$ teaspoon ground nutmeg**
> **1 teaspoon chopped chives**
> **1 cup pumpkin, cut into strips, blanched**

method
1. Bring a large saucepan of water to the boil, add fettuccine and cook until just tender. Drain.
2. Meanwhile heat cream in a large deep frying pan until reduced by half.
3. Whisk in mashed pumpkin, pepper and nutmeg, gently stir in chives and pumpkin strips.
4. Add fettuccine and toss gently. Serve immediately.

....
Serves 4

tip from the chef
Even though this dish is ideal for vegetarians, those who eat meat can add 2 spoonfuls of fried bacon cubes to the sauce.

penne
with spicy sauce

■□□ | Cooking time: 25 minutes - Preparation time: 5 minutes

method

1. Cook pasta in boiling water in a large saucepan following packet directions. Drain and keep warm.
2. To make sauce, heat oil in a frying pan over a medium heat, add onions and garlic and cook, stirring, for 5 minutes or until onions soften slightly.
3. Add cumin and chili powder and cook, stirring, for 2 minutes. Add tomatoes and black pepper to taste, bring to simmering and simmer for 6-8 minutes or until sauce thickens and tomatoes are cooked. Stir in parsley.
4. Spoon sauce over pasta and toss to combine.

....
Serves 4

ingredients

> **375 g/12 oz penne**

spicy tomato sauce
> **1 tablespoon olive oil**
> **2 onions, chopped**
> **1 clove garlic, crushed**
> **1 teaspoon ground cumin**
> **1/2 teaspoon chili powder**
> **1 kg/2 lb ripe tomatoes, peeled and chopped**
> **freshly ground black pepper**
> **2 tablespoons chopped fresh parsley**

tip from the chef
Use Italian tomatoes when in season for the best flavor and a smoother consistency.

polenta
with bolognese

■■□ | Cooking time: 75 minutes - Preparation time: 20 minutes

ingredients
> **3 cups milk**
> **3 cups water**
> **3 teaspoons salt**
> **2 cups polenta**
> **1 cup freshly grated Parmesan cheese**
> **1 tablespoon butter**
> **1 onion, chopped**
> **2 cloves garlic, crushed**
> **500 g/1 lb veal mince**
> **1 cup dry white wine**
> **1 tablespoon dried basil**
> **1¹/2 cups canned tomatoes**
> **1 cup tomato purée**
> **2 tablespoons tomato paste**
> **2 tablespoons Worcestershire sauce**

method
1. Combine milk and water in a large saucepan, add salt and bring to the boil; reduce heat and simmer. Very slowly pour polenta (a) into simmering mixture, stirring very quickly. Cook, stirring constantly, for 15 minutes.
2. Remove from heat, stir in cheese and pour polenta into a foil-lined and greased 20 cm/8 in removable base flan tin (b). Bake in a moderate oven for 20 minutes.
3. Melt butter in a large saucepan over moderate heat. Add onion and garlic, cook for 2 minutes. Add veal and brown it (c). Add wine and cook over high heat for 10 minutes. Add basil, tomatoes, tomato purée, tomato paste and Worcestershire sauce. Simmer for 25 minutes, stirring occasionally.
4. Serve Bolognese over a slice of polenta.

....
Serves 6-8

tip from the chef
Do not hesitate in trying this classic Italian dish with a full-bodied red wine.

a

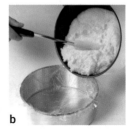
b

c

fish
with bean salad

■□□ I Cooking time: 10 minutes - Preparation time: 25 minutes

method

1. Dredge fillets in flour, then eggs, then breadcrumbs.
2. Melt butter in a large frying pan over moderate heat, add fillets and cook for 3-5 minutes each side or until cooked through. Serve immediately, with salad.
3. To make salad, in a large bowl combine chickpeas, beans, tomatoes, basil and orange rind, mix well. In a small bowl combine oil, garlic and juices, mix well and pour over salad.

Serves 4

ingredients

> **8 whiting fillets, 60 g/ 2 oz each**
> **3/4 cup flour**
> **2 eggs, beaten**
> **1 cup breadcrumbs**
> **125 g/4 oz butter**

bean salad

> **3/4 cup chickpeas, cooked**
> **1 cup green beans, cut into 2 cm/3/4 in lengths, cooked**
> **1/2 cup quartered cherry tomatoes**
> **2 tablespoons chopped basil**
> **1 tablespoon orange rind, thin strips**
> **3 tablespoons olive oil**
> **1 clove garlic, crushed**
> **1 tablespoon each freshly squeezed lime, lemon and orange juice**

tip from the chef

Another tempting option for the salad dressing is to blend 1 tablespoon mustard with 1 teaspoon sugar, 1 chopped garlic clove, 4 tablespoons balsamic vinegar and 3 tablespoons olive oil.

bream
fillets with grapes

■□□ | Cooking time: 10 minutes - Preparation time: 5 minutes

ingredients

> **4 tablespoons butter**
> **4 bream fillets, 200g/ 6$^1/_2$ oz each**
> **$^1/_2$ cup sliced button mushrooms**
> **24 seedless grapes**
> **$^1/_2$ cup sour cream**
> **$^1/_4$ cup mayonnaise**

method

1. Melt butter in a medium frying pan over moderate heat. Add fish fillets and cook for 3 minutes each side or until just cooked, remove from pan and keep warm in a low oven.

2. Add mushrooms to the frying pan and sauté over medium heat for 1 minute. Add grapes, sour cream and mayonnaise, mix well and cook until just heated through. Serve over fish fillets.

....
Serves 4

tip from the chef
Steamed green beans or boiled potatoes sprinkled with chopped dill are excellent side dishes for this fish dish.

bourride

■ ■ □ I Cooking time: 20 minutes - Preparation time: 20 minutes

method

1. Heat butter in a large saucepan over moderate heat. Add onions and parsnips; cook for 2 minutes, stirring constantly.
2. Add stock, wine, lime juice, pepper, gemfish and mussels and bring to the boil. Reduce heat to a simmer and cook until shells open.
3. Remove vegetables, gemfish and mussels from pan with a slotted spoon; remove flesh from mussel shells; reserve.
4. Add sour cream to stock mixture in pan, simmer until reduced by half and sauce begins to thicken.
5. Add reserved vegetables and seafood to sauce, stir in dill and serve.

Serves 4

ingredients

> 4 tablespoons butter
> 2 onions, sliced
> 2 parsnips, sliced
> 4 cups chicken or seafood stock
> 1 cup white wine
> 4 tablespoons freshly squeezed lime juice
> 1 teaspoon cracked black pepper
> 400 g/13 oz gemfish fillets, cut into large chunks
> 400 g/13 oz mussels, scrubbed and beards removed
> 4 tablespoons sour cream
> 1 1/2 tablespoon chopped fresh dill

tip from the chef

This recipe works great as a side dish for spaghetti if parsnips are not included.

jewfish kebabs
with sesame sauce

■□□ | Cooking time: 15 minutes - Preparation time: 15 minutes

ingredients

> **500 g/1 lb jewfish cutlets**
> **2 cloves garlic, crushed**
> **$1/4$ cup freshly squeezed lime juice**
> **3 tablespoons sesame seeds**
> **4 tablespoons olive oil**
> **1 cup cherry tomatoes**

sesame sauce

> **3 tablespoons butter**
> **1 onion, finely chopped**
> **1 teaspoon ground cumin**
> **1 teaspoon ground coriander**
> **$1/4$ cup sweet sherry**
> **3 tablespoon tahini**
> **1 tablespoon honey**
> **2 tablespoons peanut butter**
> **1 tablespoon freshly squeezed lime juice**
> **$1/4$ cup water**

method

1. Remove fish flesh from bones and cut into 2 cm/$3/4$ in cubes. Roll in combined garlic, lime juice, sesame seeds and oil and marinate for 30 minutes.
2. Thread fish and tomatoes alternately onto skewers, cook under moderate hot grill for 3 minutes each side, basting regularly with the marinade.
3. To make sauce, melt butter in a medium saucepan over moderate heat. Add onion, cumin, coriander, sherry, tahini, honey, peanut butter, lime juice and water; cook for 5 minutes stirring constantly until sauce thickens. Serve with kebabs.

....
Serves 4

tip from the chef
A simple bowl of white rice and a green salad turn these kebabs into a complete meal.

sweet
chicken drumsticks

■□□ | Cooking time: 20 minutes - Preparation time: 10 minutes

method

1. Brush each drumstick with jam (a), then roll in the flour.
2. Coat drumsticks with beaten eggs (b), then roll in the combined extra flour, salt and polenta, coat well.
3. Deep-fry drumsticks (c) until golden and cooked through, about 20 minutes.

ingredients

> **8 drumsticks**
> **1/4 cup apricot jam**
> **1 cup plain flour**
> **2 eggs, beaten**
> **1/2 cup flour, extra**
> **1 teaspoon salt**
> **3/4 cup polenta**
> **oil for deep-frying**

....
Serves 4

tip from the chef
Serve drumsticks with an orange and onion salad and you will not regret.

a   b   c

chicken thighs
with peanut sauce

■□□ | Cooking time: 30 minutes - Preparation time: 10 minutes

ingredients
> **3 tablespoons butter**
> **4 chicken thighs**
> **¹/4 cup peanut butter**
> **¹/4 cup water**
> **3 tablespoons sherry**
> **2 teaspoons grated ginger**
> **1 clove garlic, crushed**
> **¹/2 cup peanuts**
> **1 teaspoon ground cumin**
> **¹/2 cup coconut milk**
> **2 tablespoons freshly squeezed lime juice**
> **1 teaspoon mild curry powder**
> **1 tablespoon fruit chutney**
> **1 tablespoon honey**

method
1. Melt butter in a large frying pan over moderate heat. Add chicken thighs, cook until golden on each side, about 5 minutes. Transfer chicken to an ovenproof dish and bake in a moderate oven for 15 minutes or until cooked through.
2. Blend or process peanut butter, water, sherry, ginger, garlic, peanuts, cumin, coconut milk, lime juice, curry powder, chutney and honey until ingredients are combined and peanuts are finely chopped. Transfer to a medium saucepan and cook for 5 minutes over moderately low heat, stirring constantly.
3. Place chicken onto heated plates and serve with sauce.

....
Serves 4

tip from the chef
As a side dish, serve boiled rice mixed with chopped chervil or sprinkled with toasted sesame seeds.

zucchini
and chicken pancakes

■□□ | Cooking time: 15 minutes - Preparation time: 15 minutes

method

1. Blend or process flour with egg and milk until smooth. Stir in zucchini and parsley (a) and let mixture stand for 15 minutes.
2. Heat butter in a frying pan over a moderate heat. Pour about 4 tablespoons of mixture into pan and cook until golden on both sides (b). Repeat with remaining mixture.
3. Heat cream in a medium saucepan over moderate heat. Add nutmeg and wine and simmer mixture until sauce thickens slightly. Stir in chicken and chives (c), serve over pancakes.

ingredients

> 1 cup plain flour
> 1 egg
> 1 1/2 cups milk
> 1 cup grated zucchini
> 2 tablespoons chopped parsley
> 2 tablespoons butter
> 1 cup cream
> 1/4 teaspoon ground nutmeg
> 1/4 cup white wine
> 1 cup cooked chicken pieces
> 1 tablespoon chopped chives

....
Serves 4

tip from the chef

If you wish to serve these pancakes as appetizers, cook them in a small frying pan and use only 2 spoonfuls of mixture for each one. For a touch of color, add cherry tomatoes to the chicken.

a b c

corn
and cumin chicken

■□□ | Cooking time: 1 hour - Preparation time: 10 minutes

ingredients

> **1 tablespoon olive oil**
> **2 onions, chopped**
> **4 chicken thighs**
> **1 cup dry white wine**
> **1 cup chicken stock**
> **1 cup thickened cream**
> **1 cup sweet corn kernels**
> **1 tablespoon ground cumin**

method

1. Heat oil in a large frying pan over moderate heat. Add onions and cook for 2 minutes. Add chicken and sauté until golden brown, about 8 minutes. Drain chicken on absorbent kitchen paper and transfer to an ovenproof dish.
2. Pour off fat from pan and add wine. Bring to a boil over moderately high heat, scraping up the brown bits from the bottom of the pan. Boil until wine is reduced by half, about 4 minutes.
3. Stir in chicken stock, cream, corn and cumin and cook for another 5 minutes. Pour mixture over chicken in the ovenproof dish and bake in a moderate oven for 35 minutes.

....
Serves 4

tip from the chef
Stir-fried fresh vegetables are a good complement for this dish.

turkey croquettes

■ ■ □ | Cooking time: 15 minutes - Preparation time: 15 minutes

method

1. Melt butter in a medium saucepan over moderate heat. Stir in flour and cook for 30 seconds, stirring constantly. Whisk in hot milk and stir until mixture is very thick. Remove from heat.
2. Stir in ricotta cheese, turkey, Cheddar cheese and parsley, mix well and set aside until cold.
3. Divide mixture into about 1/2-cup quantities and roll into a log shape, about 10 cm/4 in length. Roll each croquette in flour, then coat with egg and roll in breadcrumbs.
4. Deep-fry croquettes for about 4 minutes or until golden.

ingredients

> **4 tablespoons butter**
> **4 tablespoons flour**
> **1 cup hot milk**
> **1/2 cup crumbled ricotta cheese**
> **3/4 cup chopped turkey**
> **1/2 cup grated Cheddar cheese**
> **2 tablespoons chopped parsley**
> **1 cup plain flour, extra**
> **1 egg, lightly beaten**
> **1 cup dried breadcrumbs**
> **oil for deep-frying**

....
Serves 4

tip from the chef
Serve as a starter or light meal, with a tossed green salad.

quick
veal stir-fry

■□□ | Cooking time: 10 minutes - Preparation time: 15 minutes

ingredients
> **2 tablespoons oil**
> **350 g/11 oz veal fillets, cut into thin strips**
> **1 onion, sliced**
> **1 red pepper, seeded and cut into thin strips**
> **1 tablespoon honey**
> **1 tablespoon brown sugar**
> **1/4 cup white wine**
> **1/4 cup freshly squeezed lemon juice**
> **1 cup drained baby sweet corn cobs**
> **100 g/31/2 oz snow peas, trimmed**
> **1 tablespoon chopped dill**

method
1. Heat oil in a medium frying pan over moderate heat. Add veal, onion and pepper, cook for 3 minutes or until veal is cooked. Remove from pan and set aside.
2. Add honey, sugar, wine and lemon juice to pan and cook for 3 minutes.
3. Add corn, snow peas, dill, veal, onion and pepper to pan and toss well. Serve immediately.

....
Serves 4

tip from the chef
Serve with braised halved fennel bulbs as a side dish.

veal bundles

■■□ | Cooking time: 10 minutes - Preparation time: 15 minutes

method

1. In a blender or food processor finely chop mozzarella cheese, bacon and parsley (a). Transfer to a bowl, mix in Parmesan cheese.
2. Divide mixture in four; lay each veal fillet flat and spoon mixture on top. Roll up and secure bundles with string (b), roll bundles in flour.
3. Heat oil in a large frying pan over moderate heat. Add bundles and brown. Add wine (c) and cook for 5 minutes. Remove string, strain pan juices and pour over bundles; serve immediately.

ingredients

> 75 g/2¹/2 oz mozzarella cheese, grated
> 75 g/2¹/2 oz bacon, rind removed
> 2 tablespoons chopped parsley
> 2 tablespoons Parmesan cheese
> 4 veal fillets, 75 g/ 2¹/2 oz each, pounded
> ¹/2 cup plain flour
> 4 tablespoons oil
> ³/4 cup white wine

....
Serves 4

tip from the chef

Accompany with baked sweet potatoes and potatoes.

a

b

c

tomato
steak casserole

■ ■ ☐ I Cooking time: 95 minutes - Preparation time: 15 minutes

ingredients

> **200 g/6$^1/_2$ oz pork rind**
> **2 tablespoons olive oil**
> **1 onion, chopped**
> **2 cloves garlic, crushed**
> **500 g/1 lb baby potatoes, halved**
> **1 kg/2 lb chuck steak, fat removed, cut into large chunks**
> **2 cups red wine**
> **1$^1/_2$ cups canned tomatoes**
> **2 tablespoons tomato paste**
> **3 cups chicken stock**
> **1 cup sliced celery**
> **1 tablespoon chopped parsley**

method

1. Bring water to the boil in a large saucepan, add pork rind and cook for 2 minutes; drain and cut into thin strips; set aside.
2. Heat oil in a large flameproof casserole dish over moderate heat. Add onion, garlic and potatoes, cook for 7 minutes, stirring constantly.
3. Add steak pieces and pork rind, brown on all sides. Add wine, tomatoes, tomato paste and stock. Bring to the boil, reduce heat, cover and simmer for 1$^1/_4$ hours, stirring occasionally.
4. Draw off as much fat as possible, stir in celery and parsley and serve.

....
Serves 8

tip from the chef
Decorate with a bunch of fresh parsley and serve in the same casserole dish.

pork spareribs with pear sauce

■□□ | Cooking time: 55 minutes - Preparation time: 10 minutes

method

1. Melt butter in a large frying pan over moderate heat. Add spareribs, ginger and sugar, cook until ribs are golden on each side. Transfer ribs to an ovenproof dish and bake in a moderate oven for 45 minutes.

2. Meanwhile, pour excess fat from frying pan, add pear syrup and cook over moderate heat until sauce thickens, about 7 minutes. Cut each pear half into 4 slices and add to the sauce.

3. When spareribs are cooked, add to the sauce and stir. Serve garnished with orange rind and watercress sprigs.

ingredients

> **4 tablespoons butter**
> **4 pork spareribs, halved**
> **1 tablespoon grated ginger**
> **2 tablespoons brown sugar**
> **425 g/13½ oz canned pear halves and syrup**
> **1 tablespoon orange rind, thin strips**
> **watercress sprigs to garnish**

....
Serves 4

tip from the chef
If you don't have brown sugar, you can use honey instead.

coconut
lamb satay

■□□ | Cooking time: 10 minutes - Preparation time: 10 minutes

ingredients
> **500 g/1 lb lamb mince**
> **1 tablespoon tomato paste**
> **3 tablespoons desiccated coconut**
> **1 teaspoon ground cumin**
> **2 tablespoons chopped fresh coriander**
> **1 tablespoon chopped fresh parsley**
> **3 tablespoons freshly squeezed lime juice**

method
1. In a large bowl combine mince, tomato paste, coconut, cumin, coriander, parsley and lime juice, mix well (a).
2. Roll tablespoons of mixture into balls and place 3 balls on each skewer (b).
3. Cook satay under a moderate grill for about 3 minutes on each side or until cooked through (c).

....
Serves 4-6

tip from the chef
For a hot touch, add 1 teaspoon grated fresh ginger to the mixture.

a

b

c

lamb
patties with chutney

■□□ I Cooking time: 20 minutes - Preparation time: 10 minutes

method

1. In a large bowl combine lamb with onion, breadcrumbs and tomato paste, mix well. Shape into 2 cm/3/4 in thick patties and grill under a moderate heat for about 5 minutes each side or until cooked through.
2. Meanwhile melt butter in a medium saucepan over moderate heat, add extra onion, salt and pepper, cook for 1 minute. Stir in sugar, vinegar and mint. Simmer for 3 minutes, stirring constantly. Add water and simmer until mixture is slightly thickened.
3. Serve patties with chutney.

ingredients

> 500 g/1 lb lamb mince
> 1 onion, finely chopped
> 3 tablespoons breadcrumbs
> 1 tablespoon tomato paste
> 3 tablespoons butter
> 1 onion, extra, chopped
> salt and freshly ground pepper
> 3 teaspoons brown sugar
> 3 tablespoons white wine vinegar
> 1/2 teaspoon finely chopped mint
> 1/4 cup water

....
Serves 4

tip from the chef

For variation, replace lamb mince with a mix of beef and pork mince in equal parts.

frankfurt
casserole

■□□ | Cooking time: 50 minutes - Preparation time: 10 minutes

ingredients
> 3 tablespoons butter
> 1 onion, chopped
> 1 cup sliced mushrooms
> 1/4 cup chopped bacon, rind removed
> 1 cup barley, soaked for 2 hours, drained
> 3 cups chicken stock
> 3/4 cup dry white wine
> 1 teaspoon ground cumin
> 1/2 teaspoon ground coriander
> 1/2 cup cream
> 500 g/1 lb thin frankfurters, cut into 2 cm/3/4 in lengths

method
1. Melt butter in a large frying pan over moderate heat. Add onion, mushrooms and bacon, cook for 3 minutes, stirring constantly.
2. Add barley, stock, wine, cumin and coriander and simmer until stock is absorbed, about 30 minutes.
3. Stir in cream and frankfurters, cook for a further 10 minutes and serve.

....
Serves 4

tip from the chef
Recent studies have shown that barley can lower cholesterol. Beta-glucan, a type of fiber which blends with cholesterol and helps with its removal from the body, is thought to be the ingredient responsible for this.

italian
bean salad

■□□ | Cooking time: 0 minute - Preparation time: 10 minutes

method

1. In a large bowl combine butter beans, red kidney beans, mushrooms, Italian sausage and chives.

2. Mix lemon juice, olive oil, garlic and basil, and pour over salad; toss well and marinate for 1 hour before serving.

....
Serves 4

ingredients

> **1¹/4 cups canned butter beans, drained**
> **1¹/4 cups canned red kidney beans, drained**
> **100 g/3¹/2 oz button mushrooms, sliced**
> **2 sticks Italian sausage, sliced**
> **2 tablespoons chopped chives**
> **¹/4 cup freshly squeezed lemon juice**
> **4 tablespoons olive oil**
> **1 clove garlic, crushed**
> **2 teaspoons dried basil**

tip from the chef

This salad can be enriched with cubes of mozzarella cheese.

choc-orange
mousse

■ ■ □ | Cooking time: 5 minutes - Preparation time: 15 minutes

ingredients
> **4 eggs, separated**
> **1/4 cup caster sugar**
> **3 tablespoons orange juice concentrate**
> **200 g/61/2 oz dark chocolate, broken up**
> **11/2 cups cream**
> **3 tablespoons sugar, extra**

method
1. Beat egg yolks, sugar and orange juice in a small bowl with an electric mixer until creamy.
2. Place chocolate and cream in a heatproof bowl over a saucepan of simmering water. Stir constantly until chocolate has melted and combined well with cream. Beat into egg/sugar mixture and mix well.
3. In a separate bowl beat egg whites and extra sugar until soft peaks form. Fold chocolate mixture into egg whites, half a cup at a time, stir until just combined. Pour mixture into serving glasses and refrigerate 1 hour before serving.

....
Serves 4-6

tip from the chef
Decorate mousse with orange rind and fresh mint if desired or, even better, garnish with glacé orange peel.

honey *custard*

■☐☐ I Cooking time: 35 minutes - Preparation time: 15 minutes

method

1. Scald milk; do not boil. Remove from heat, stir in honey and vanilla.
2. Mix 3 tablespoons of hot milk mixture into beaten eggs, mix well. Pour egg mixture into remaining warm milk and whisk for 30 seconds.
3. Pour mixture through a sieve into four 3/4-cup capacity greased ramekins. Place ramekins in a 5 cm/2 in deep baking dish and surround with 2 cm/3/4 in deep boiling water.
4. Bake custards in a moderate oven for 30 minutes. Drizzle honey over the top of custards and sprinkle with cinnamon before serving.

ingredients

> **2 cups milk**
> **1/4 cup honey**
> **2 teaspoons vanilla essence**
> **4 eggs, beaten**
> **honey to drizzle**
> **1 teaspoon ground cinnamon**

....
Serves 4

tip from the chef

For a super attractive presentation, decorate with caramel drippings and caramelized apple slices.

orange
in wine syrup

■□□ | Cooking time: 10 minutes - Preparation time: 5 minutes

ingredients

> **6 oranges, peeled and segmented**
> **4 tablespoons honey**
> **4 tablespoons brown sugar**
> **4 tablespoons freshly squeezed lemon juice**
> **1 cup red wine**

method

1. Arrange orange segments in 4 serving glasses.
2. Heat honey, sugar, lemon juice and red wine in a large saucepan over high heat, stirring constantly. Bring to the boil, reduce heat and simmer until syrup has reduced by half and thickened slightly.
3. Pour syrup over orange segments and serve.

....

Serves 4

tip from the chef
As a great finish for a light menu, sprinkle with fresh chopped mint and serve with vanilla ice-cream.

sultana
cheesecake

■□□ | Cooking time: 1 hour - Preparation time: 10 minutes

method

1. Blend or process ricotta cheese with lemon juice, vanilla essence and sugar until smooth. While motor is running, add eggs and cinnamon (a), process for a further 1 minute.

2. Transfer mixture to a large bowl, stir in cream (b), mix well. Stir in sultanas and pour mixture into a greased and lined 22 cm/8^1/$_2$ in springform pan (c).

3. Bake cheesecake in a moderate oven for 1 hour. Let cheesecake sit for 10 minutes before removing pan.

ingredients

> **500 g/1 lb ricotta cheese**
> **juice of 1 lemon**
> **2 tablespoons vanilla essence**
> **^{1}/$_2$ cup caster sugar**
> **3 eggs**
> **1 teaspoon ground cinnamon**
> **1 cup cream**
> **1 cup sultanas**

....
Serves 6

tip from the chef

Dust cheesecake with icing sugar when cold.

a

b

c

index

Chef
express

low cost
cooking

Great tasting, delicious meals
don't need to be costly!
Turn to these
easy-to-prepare, beautifully
illustrated new recipes
for great ideas for cooking
on a budget.

$3.95 U.S./$4.95 Can.
ISBN 13: 9781582796840
ISBN 10: 158279684X

TYPHOON
MEDIA CORPORATION

50395

9 781582 796840

Chef
express

my first
cookbook